Pebble Plus
Bilingüe/Bilingual

Investiga las estaciones/Investigate the Seasons

Veamos el otoño/ Let's Look at Fall

por/by Sarah L. Schuette

Traducción/Translation: Dr. Martín Luis Guzmán Ferrer
Editor Consultor/Consulting Editor: Dra. Gail Saunders-Smith

Capstone press

Mankato, Minnesota

Pebble Plus is published by Capstone Press,
151 Good Counsel Drive, P.O. Box 669, Mankato, Minnesota 56002.
www.capstonepress.com

092010
005927R

Library of Congress Cataloging-in-Publication Data
Schuette, Sarah L., 1976–
     [Let's look at fall. Spanish & English]
     Veamos el otoño / por Sarah L. Schuette = Let's look at fall / by Sarah L. Schuette.
     p. cm. — (Pebble Plus. Investiga las estaciones = Investigate the seasons)
     Includes index.
     ISBN-13: 978-1-4296-2288-2 (hardcover)
     ISBN-13: 978-1-4296-5178-3 (paperback)
     1. Animal behavior — Juvenile literature. 2. Autumn — Juvenile literature. I. Title. II. Title:
Let's look at fall.
QL753.S3818 2009
508.2 — dc22   2008004827

Summary: Simple text and photographs present what happens to the weather, animals, and plants in fall — in
     both English and Spanish.

Editorial Credits
Martha E. H. Rustad, editor; Katy Kudela, bilingual editor; Adalín Torres-Zayas, Spanish copy editor;
     Bobbi J. Wyss, set designer; Veronica Bianchini, book designer; Kara Birr, photo researcher;
     Scott Thoms, photo editor

Photo Credits
Corbis/Donna Disario, cover (background tree)
James P. Rowan, 21
Peter Arnold/Tom Vezo, 12–13
Photo Researchers, Inc/James Zipp, 7
PhotoEdit Inc./Dennis MacDonald, 18–19
Shutterstock/Alphonse Tran, 9; bora ucak, cover, 1 (magnifying glass); Elena Elisseeva, 5; Stuart Blyth, cover
     (leaf inset); Wesley Aston, 14–15
SuperStock/age fotostock, 11; Steve Vidler, 16–17
UNICORN Stock Photos/Robert Hitchman, 1 (rake)

The author dedicates this book to her Grandma Minnie Simcox of Belle Plaine, Minnesota.

Note to Parents and Teachers

The Investiga las estaciones/Investigate the Seasons set supports national science standards related to weather and climate. This book describes and illustrates fall in both English and Spanish. The images support early readers in understanding the text. The repetition of words and phrases helps early readers learn new words. This book also introduces early readers to subject-specific vocabulary words, which are defined in the Glossary section. Early readers may need assistance to read some words and to use the Table of Contents, Glossary, Internet Sites, and Index sections of the book.

Table of Contents

Tabla de contenidos

It's Fall!

How do you know it's fall?

A cool breeze blows.

The weather is colder.

¡Es otoño!

¿Cómo sabemos que es otoño?

Sopla una brisa fresca.

El clima es más frío.

Leaves change color.
They flutter to
the ground.

Las hojas cambian de
color y revolotean
en el suelo.

The sun sets earlier.
Fall days are shorter
than summer days.

El Sol se pone más
temprano. Los días de
otoño son más cortos
que los de verano.

Animals in Fall

What do animals do in fall?
Squirrels rush around. They
gather nuts to store for winter.

Los animales en otoño

¿Qué es lo que hacen los animales
en otoño? Las ardillas corretean.
Juntan nueces y las guardan
para el invierno.

Birds fly south.
They look for
warmer weather.

Los pájaros vuelan al
sur. Buscan un clima
más templado.

Bears search for a place
to hibernate. Their fur
coats grow thicker.

Los osos buscan un lugar
para hibernar. Su pelo
se pone más tupido.

Plants in Fall

What happens to plants
in fall? Ripe apples fill
the orchard. They're ready
to be picked.

Las plantas en otoño

¿Qué les pasa a las plantas
en otoño? La huerta se
llena de manzanas maduras.
Están listas para recogerse.

Corn ripens in the
field. It's ready to
be harvested.

El maíz se madura en
los campos. Está listo
para cosecharse.

What's Next?

The temperature grows

cold. Fall is over.

What season is next?

¿Qué le sigue?

El clima es cada vez más

frío. Ha terminado el otoño.

¿Cuál es la siguiente estación?

Glossary

breeze — a gentle wind

flutter — to wave, flap, or float in a breeze; leaves flutter as they drop off tree branches.

harvest — to gather crops that are ready to be picked; fall is a time for harvesting crops such as corn, soybeans, wheat, and oats.

hibernate — to spend the winter in a deep sleep

orchard — a field or farm where fruit trees grow

ripen — to become ready to be picked

season — one of the four parts of the year; winter, spring, summer, and fall are seasons.

weather — the condition outdoors at a certain time and place; weather changes with each season.

Glosario

la **brisa** — un viento suave

el **clima** — las condiciones a la intemperie en cierta época del año o lugar; el clima cambia con cada estación.

cosechar — reunir los cultivos que están listos para recogerse; el otoño es el la época del año para cosechar cultivos como el maíz, la soya, el trigo y la avena.

la **estación** — una de las cuatro épocas del año; el invierno, la primavera, el verano y el otoño son estaciones.

hibernar — pasar el invierno en un sueño profundo

la **huerta** — campo o granja donde crecen árboles frutales

madurar — estar listo para cosecharse

revolotear — agitarse, aletear o flotar en la brisa; las hojas flotan cuando se caen de los ramas de los árboles.

Internet Sites

FactHound offers a safe, fun way to find Internet sites related to this book. All of the sites on FactHound have been researched by our staff.

Here's how:

1. Visit *www.facthound.com*

2. Choose your grade level.

3. Type in this book ID **1429622881** for age-appropriate sites. You may also browse subjects by clicking on letters, or by clicking on pictures and words.

4. Click on the **Fetch It** button.

FactHound will fetch the best sites for you!

Index

Sitios de Internet

FactHound te brinda una manera divertida y segura de encontrar sitios de Internet relacionados con este libro. Hemos investigado todos los sitios de FactHound. Es posible que algunos sitios no estén en español.

Se hace así:

1. Visita *www.facthound.com*

2. Elige tu grado escolar.

3. Introduce este código especial **1429622881** para ver sitios apropiados a tu edad, o usa una palabra relacionada con este libro para hacer una búsqueda general.

4. Haz un clic en el botón **Fetch It**.

¡FactHound buscará los mejores sitios para ti!

Índice